D1566033

Twice Removed

ALSO BY RALPH ANGEL

Neither World
Anxious Latitudes

Twice Removed

POEMS Ralph Angel

Sarabande  Books
LOUISVILLE, KENTUCKY

No part of this book may be reproduced without written permission of
the publisher. Please direct inquiries to:

Managing Editor
Sarabande Books, Inc.
2234 Dundee Road, Suite 200
Louisville, KY 40205

LIBRARY OF CONGRESS CATALOGING–IN–PUBLICATION DATA

Angel, Ralph, 1951–
    Twice removed : poems / by Ralph Angel. — 1st ed.
        p.   cm.
    ISBN 1-889330-57-4 (cloth : alk. paper) — ISBN 1-889330-58-2
(pbk. : alk. paper)
    I. Title.
PS3551.N457 T9 2001
811'.54—dc21   2001017011

Cover photograph: "Le Dôme, boulevard Montparnasse. Juin 1925" by
Eugéne Atget. Albumen-silver print from glass negative, 7 x 9⅜" (18 x 24
cm). The Museum of Modern Art, New York. Abbott-Levy Collection.
Partial gift of Shirley C. Burden. Print by Chicago Albumen Works, 1984.
Copy Print © 2000 The Museum of Modern Art, New York.

Cover and text design by Charles Casey Martin.

Manufactured in the United States of America.
This book is printed on acid-free paper.

Sarabande Books is a nonprofit literary organization.

Funded in part by a grant from the Kentucky Arts Council, a state
agency of the Education, Arts and Humanities Cabinet, and by a grant
from the National Endowment for the Arts.

for Debra

CONTENTS

ACKNOWLEDGMENTS

Acknowledgment is made to the following publications for poems which originally appeared in them:

The American Poetry Review: "Breathing Out," "Decalogue," "Even Because," "Interior Landscape," "It Takes a While to Disappear," "Like Animals," "The Nothing That Is," "The Vigil," "Tidy," "Twilight," "Untitled," "You Think It's a Secret But It Never Was One"

The American Voice: "Months Later"

Colorado Review: "A Waltz for Debbie," "Silk," "The Local Language," "Untitled"

Denver Quarterly: "A Second Silence," "And More," "Between Murmur and Glare"

Faultline: "Late for Work"

Harvard Review: "Cul-de-sac"

Interim: "Such Weather"

Kestrel: "Kapparah," "There Was a Silence"

Poetry: "And So Asks," "Half Circle," "In the Calm," "This"

Third Coast: "Alpine Wedding," "From the Balcony"

Volt: "Twice Removed"

"Twice Removed" also appeared in *The Pushcart Prize XIX: Best of the Small Presses*

"The Nothing That Is" and "Twilight" also appeared in *The Body Electric*

"Untitled" also appeared in *Anthology of Magazine Verse & Yearbook of American Poetry*

"Decalogue" is for Krzyztof Kieslowski

"Interior Landscape" is for Helen Frankenthaler

And the blood of desire
which changes from nature
images images
without a single reality
to feed it
　　　　　—Pierre Reverdy

Twice Removed

Not even sleep (though I'm ashamed of that too).
Or watching my sleeping self drift out and kick harder, burst
       awake, and then the nothing,
leaf-shadow, a shave and
black coffee, I know how a dream sounds.

This ease. This difficulty. The brain that lives on a little longer.
       The long
commute (not even what happened back then—this sort of
giving up with no one around and therefore
no charge for anything).

No word. No feeling
when a feeling wells up and is that much further.
Cupola and drumming, from the inside, holes open up a sky
       no thicker than cardboard.
You, the one I'd step over. You, whom I care for

and lie to, who doesn't want to, either, not even this failure
(having grown so used to it), the wreck that still
seeps from a stone, sinks down among the roots and, in that
       perfect darkness, such bloom.
No name for it. No place inscribed with its own grief,

where the grass resists, and I too

resist.

No place to get to. No place to leave from. No place where
     those times,

and times like these, are allowed to die.

Months Later

Where? In the black trees that lay down and drown here? In
    the drowned clouds?—and no one to hold them back.
    Rhododendron, the night never ends. A still-life and a
    way to get home again. A moss-dark photograph turned
    holy in his memory.

It's anyone against the wind tonight. In the eyes of a child
    who looks up at us from the bottom of a well, or across
    the table, the uninvited guest taking the oranges we
    intended to eat.

In these very hands. A window of the soul already open to
    the sea. An hour outside of itself. A name that's repeated
    over and over until it's just noise.

River of ashes. River and flame, the small vibration we set in
    motion there. I wouldn't know how to find you or
    anyone.

Searchlights and choppers. With cats on the rooftops and moths-
    turned-to-dust on the sill. Pillar, and bell tower. Wall, and
    earlier than that, the peaceful cities.

Calm, without talking. In our oldest clothes. From the
    balcony, on the fire escape—just leaning on the railings
    above the flooded streets.

The Nothing That Is

That there was later on
among the tables and the tents of swirling light
the most exotic chill of laughter,
wrists, and touchable,
the need to touch and hear the distance,
umbrella damp, the last few
ugly words come back to pain
already lifted.

Not answering.
Not answering and, therefore,
not alone, double-fisted, this public
alley, this private wooden desk and room,
the cards and letters
I'm afraid of.

That there was later still,
but briefer, another cover, another
leap of faith and most of us, the untouched
sand and ether. Not you,
but blankly. Not her,
the looping swallows, the muffled eaves.
In the liquid light of traffic,
jasmine, cough and shatter. The hand
pressed close.
The mere sensation.

The Local Language

The way she puts her fingers to his chest when she greets him.

The way an old man quiets himself,

or that another man waits, and waits a long time, before
     speaking.
It's in the gaze that steadies, a music

he grows into—something about
Mexico, I imagine, how he first learned about light there.

It's in the blank face of every child,
a water that stands still amid the swirling current,

water breaking apart as it leaves the cliff and falls forever
through its own, magnificent window.

The way a young woman holds out a cupped hand, and doves
     come to her.

The way a man storms down the street as if to throw open
     every door.

And the word she mouths to herself as she looks up from her
     book—for
that word, as she repeats it,

repeats it.

Late for Work

In the throes
of winter a tropical storm muddies
the gutters

where traffic congests and then as always
eases us through.

Maybe I knelt there
for since they have vanished the lamps
in shop windows

flicker within. Somebody
flinching. A red
umbrella and that part of town swept from the hip

and the shoulder.
From my

open side. Somebody
pushing a bicycle. Somebody's alone
on the square.

So much
springtime we slog to catch up
to that first wave

of heat. People chatting
and murmuring. A young man

pouring tea.
The way an old man dabs his wet face
with a napkin. The way

she reclines when she reads.
So much cinnamon
and bread.

God how I love Darjeeling.

And More

I open my eyes again. So be it,
good. Don't leave. The dark slides into slippers
easily. The quiet finds a robe. The room
rises and is falling with your
breathing. As if
I'd never seen you sleeping,
in this house and warmth,
at this hour, this bed
I can't quite
put my finger on
and like.

Breathing Out

Now you are crossing a wide street at night
anxious in the traffic and rushing
to get to the bakery
before closing. What could be more breathtaking
than your beauty if not in my arms
at least on that side
of peril. That's
why I'm yelling at the driver of the pickup truck
I just slammed into so much did I
want to park there and
wait for you.

May I never live with love
by surviving love and loving blocks and days away
the most ancient of the dead desire earthly
our getting born again
alone without
choice

children fill the air
the spices and the rugs of the bazaar.

I buy you tulips.
They are yellow and bright.
The port is dark and glittering blue airplanes
hover there. Like clarity
itself. Like
faintly wailing sirens attached to absolutely

nothing.
Like socks and sweaters and
the blanket that slipped somehow
from your legs while I
tidied up the balcony so lost in your book
are you tonight.

Even Because

Because it all just breaks apart, and the pieces scatter and
      rearrange without much fanfare or notice.

Because you can't and don't remember the step that kicked up
      dust and left this planet—you'd give up even more now.

Because the body itself—the heart's

not dead but deeper, wrapped up in curtains, a different color,
      among the railings and the pigeons, the rooftops and
      walls—

for all you know it's a question of bread

or beer.

Because even love

returns. The city's all brightness

and shadow, deckle-edged, bluer than air—there's no help
      anywhere—you no longer know how to listen.

And love says, love—midnight to midnight,

already ablaze. And the boulevard—wide-open. And the well-
stocked crowdless market, and a lone taxi blears.

Even happiness—the way anger's come back to roost again.
And joy, though joy's not in the ear or the eye. On this
walk

the gulls hover offshore and the islands are speckled with fire.

Even love, even because.

There Was a Silence

and then a greater more
unnerving will to laugh out loud,

a slashing rain
and then that moment in traffic when the dull

thud of windshield wipers
wholly isolates you,

when into a corner booth the raised
eyebrows of evening glimmer in our knowing,

photographs are taken—
you still feel dirty.

Untitled

A poem begins.
People are walking down the street.
A few of them step into a doorway and light cigarettes.
A silhouette turns in a hotel-lobby window toward your
      reflection.
Everything hurries to make room for you.
You and all those you love and no longer know or grieve for
      and wish were here.
Enters your room and sits down.

A stick figure tosses a hat from the bridge.
A girl child crawls out of a cardboard box and cracks herself up.
Two hands clapping.
Is there not among the tables a waiter

already there?
The hollow sound of waves and a shopkeeper sweeping?
A woman dining alone?

They say that these scarves are among the finest in the world.
The purest water anywhere.
Adorn yourself.
Luxuriate.
The birds have fashioned the trees.
From a bench in the shade a couple looks out from a dream.
Vendors of ice cream

and baskets.

It is your eyes they look into.

Even the one who closes his own to hear himself singing.

In the Calm

and the clear, I found a way back to my body. The snake
    danced with the birds and the branches. Her loose shirt
    made a rhythm of waves. And when I awakened

buildings blushed with kisses and the flutterings of wings.
    Everything was silent, for once, in the ground. Certain
    skies

departed. A guitar sang from a narrow street—footsteps rose
    and turned—in the open windows the ghosts of silk-
    dyers let down their hair.

In the dead swirl of air we were all together. Stone by stone,
    the tiniest hill made us twilight. Fireflies ignited

and the smoke was fragrant with scallions and roasted potatoes.
    Dogs played like flowers. Grown-ups in black, grown-
    ups in costume. And we kids

tried to laugh even louder, so loudly our lungs and bug-eyes
    and weakening throats sounded something like unheard-
    of distance

and real laughter, and, when I woke up, the really real.

Kapparah

But to make this ugly
we'd have to undo even the hours
of this room.
And many years earlier
the unsaid
will flop like a fish
and in the morning step out
on the balcony.
All the way
to nothing drifting.
A view much like our own.
A plan.

We'd have to
think desire could be practiced
and fail and
study constantly
and know by heart
the volumes of our mingled
vast migrations
and the trampled starts
of things.
We were holy places there.
And we would keep
repeating that.

A Second Silence

I'll rely, then, upon the drumming.
My face. This voice. Demons that belong to me only. The dog
that ripped my fucking arm off and bounded away.
He just wants to play, to free the hissing
sprinklers from the grounds
of the estate.

I used to fear my neighbors, too, until
they stormed the canyon and torched the place. It's all
mud with light now, a second silence,
a towering, broken
tree.

I'll ask for hunger. It's here. My nakedness
and shame. The city washes over. The suburbs filthy clean.
For sleeplessness, everyone's

alone. Every one of us
dies young.

As in a dream,
only wind and sky. One's village and oneself.
The stones. The rind.

Untitled

Or as along the river buildings brighten and grow dim again.
As a distant bridge repeats itself, and the domes above, and that
    much further, the city reassembled there.

Easy as listening, or choosing not to. A breeze comes up, a
    door glides
through its own perfect outline. Halyards and traffic. In a
    courtyard the puddles of last night's rain.

I watched my pain ease between spaces of the air itself.
Watched a waiter fidget with his apron, a woman selling lilacs,
    arranging cans. Strangers, their footsteps, as if

the soul were buoyed there, moist and leafy, a shadowed street
    where fruit rots in a wooden crate.
A pile of bricks. A ladder. Packages and papers, I miss everyone.

As in this quiet, always. My body. A whispered song.
As if, in this quiet, a man turns away and with a pole a
    shopkeeper lowers the awnings.

My body. In time. And the hour passes.

Like Animals

To give birth to ourselves each day makes this death
an act of will, and stopping here to say goodbye is all too sadly
        telling.
The air is limned with secrets, and we are painted tenderly,
and awkward. A breeze stirs up our alibis, but
they can be rewritten, and later still the fact of our desire.
It's enough to kiss the surface, a twitch
distinguished from afar, the regions
of our sufferings mapped out upon a sleeve.
Enough that nothing's missing, that the chapters
line up perfectly, how once revealed we
never stop reacting, how we
become the only character, looking
upward, tying a shoe.

Half Circle

Your body has recovered you.
Fog, or stars, a leaf of spring, the little
veins you're tracing, the world's
still healthy here.
And mother's well, though
you're her sister now.
The man who always loved you
thinks he's free. The woman
who loved your husband
wants your sympathy.
And lawyers come.
Accountants.
You can talk to them
at least, and do, the way
the city's here.

A rock's thrown
through the window.
A man's beaten in the hall.
The same young woman, night to night,
sleeps against your door.
The man who always loved you
thinks that you
belong to him. The woman
who loved your husband
counts you as a friend.
A new neighbor
phones. Bankers

call. Even the girl who
stole your purse tracks you down.
You can't accept, of course.
Her need is greater.

It Takes a While to Disappear

The city purrs, it hums along, the morning hardly risen.
A well-dressed drunk smears her finger across a doorman's lips
    and whispers.
Someone stumbles. Someone curses. Someone hoses down
    the pavement.
We must have made a mess of things again, all fuzzy black and
    white
and greenish at the corners. Some final thing
that put us in our places.

You're still standing in your winter coat alongside
everything you wanted and deserve. But you were thinner.
    The desk clerk
looked right through you. The cabby didn't listen. You were
out of sorts back then, you say, but
you're still frowning!

In vain a shrieking siren repeats itself
and fades. The quiet idles there, a crosswalk signal chirping.
    You're still
standing in your winter coat, but I don't know you. Someone
scrambles down a fire escape, his shirt a flag
that's shredded. A boy

salutes. And then his mother, too.

She stoops to smooth his collar. She makes a sculpture of her
      packages.

You're a different person now, you say, but

you will never happen.

Such Weather

What with her looking away, him not even trying...

A few strangers, too, get caught—oblivious, hollow-eyed,
their mouths set in stone...

You'd think that time as it freezes would be kinder than that.
He'll leap from a window,
                        she'll find out everything.
That the end, when the end arrives,
what an exaggeration.
                        She'll leave early and miss the train,
he'll wake up alongside a woman who loves him.

O nearness to life—
                        what with more trouble in the north, and,
in the markets, such weather.
                        Her hair will grow back,
he'll pace like his father.
                        He'll throw open his mind again,
and again she'll remember, standing
stiffly against the mirror.

Decalogue

Nothing hidden. Leaflessly grey
and cold. Only one car
below.

Nothing spared. A small boy
gently walking alone. His eyes are dark and wide open
naturally. The pond is a short cut. Its thin ice

tested by his father hours ago.

———————

Water dripping from the ceiling is the world to a man
in a coma. His wife stalks the doctor.
If he lives

she will abort the baby of her lover. He won't
and she cancels her appointment.
And he does.

———————

There now.
7 a.m. in a station is not arbitrary.
You were not alone. And at one minute past

with your gloved fingers
you let it go.

——————

A letter arrives. It was written
twenty years ago. It never need be opened.
We found it

in a drawer because
we wanted to. Because we love and we are neither
parent nor child. We wished

for the impossible.
We did not know we were impossible.

——————

A young man accepts the cigarette.
He stubs it out. When
the trapdoor

opens
his hands twitch a little.
He could not

kill the cabby with a rope. He beat his face in
with a cudgel.
On the riverbank the quiet

took its time. He crushed that man
quickly with a stone.

———————

A virgin answers all her questions.
He's in love. She's experienced. She instructs him.
They are not in her

apartment. Their
hands are not caressing. They are not excited
and do not suffer.

And oh how they've changed places.

———————

Nearly every night. For a long time
a small girl screams and

screams.

She will not reveal her nightmare.
Again the light
comes early. On mountains of animals

she sleeps soundly.
And you are frightened too.

———————

Nothing changes. It is spring. The man who
tried to save you cannot
speak.

The woman who sent you to your certain death
needs a friend. When
you pray

she prays.
Her husband turned away.
Back then the cups were of the finest china

but each was different. The oil lamp
unlit.

———————

Lushly green
and cold. They'll adopt they say.
She will end it. And she does. He doesn't

know. She'll weep the way he
wept alone. Is it you
my love?

There?

———————————

What you've achieved.
And other people's memories
of you.

You forget. It's childish
but nice.
Only money. Only

things. Your
kidney for a rose-colored stamp.
We're here

and nothing else exists.

Twilight

That he might just snap again was part of it, blind himself, and,
    well, you're there.
You'd climb the wooden stairs again, lock the bathroom door
    behind you, will yourself away.
                          Maybe get it right this
    time, I don't know,
the card I thought to send, a thousand crows on a Chinese
    screen, a light from down below somewhere, everything.

Among schools of flashing fish, a shadow and its camera, we've
    all been there before.
Among the fruit and praying figures, his latest medication, his
    threatening, stupid call, each dangerous time.
You talk to him, put aside a little money for somebody else,
    pen messages, and stay. Move again.
                        And it's a better
    story there,

it must be. The beginning of a street, a slant of houses. Glint
    and shimmerings, porches, and leaves. And now the
    twilight,
instantaneous. The tables, and the chairs. How the unseen
    break bread together, carefully.

Cul-de-sac

About as empty
as sunlight against the side of a house, an embankment
stripped of dust and graffiti.
The days are short. The shadows longer than those of summer.
    In the bright
between, a man in a blue suit rakes leaves.

And a car sputters. Doves flop into trees. An old woman
puts a cigarette to her mouth, then
turns from the window.
Up the street, houses go pale. The hill is splashed with color—
    brown
and sienna, burnt orange, grey—

the entire sky a wisp of barely blue. And in some room,
    somewhere, a neighbor
plays her piano. Two squirrels
chase and chatter, rooftop to balcony, to wire.
Incredible, the silence,
this flurry of notes that reflects it.

Interior Landscape

In the blink of an eye, a light rain.
Among the ten-thousand synapses, the sound of rain, but
      delicately, the sound of leaves.

In the blink of an eye, a pure-cold air.
Were I swimming there, how clearly I could see my hands and
      everything they touch.

Among all shapes growing here and dying, a sweet
and earthy smell. The weight and feel spread thinly, my own
      blue house below,

as if the port were sighing, the cliffs
hauled in from afar, a wave of rolling tiled roofs and lamp stain
      splashed against the walls.

In the blink of an eye, no wonder.
In the blink of an eye, an empty room. The unread paper.
      The space I've cleared.

You Think It's a Secret
But It Never Was One

You think it's a secret, but it never was.
Sell the house, move to the beach, this *isn't* his closet,
there are no phantoms here.

You think that if you know the truth you'll forgive her. "I lied,"
she said. "I was afraid, afraid I'd be left alone."

Do we not each day leave this world
together, half asleep, a goodbye kiss steadying ourselves
against the seats of the train?

Do we not meet again and, always
dreaming, *not* find a word for it, the dream that would exclude us?

Someone remembers something that happened a long time
ago. She forgot it, it changed everything.

What can I tell you that you don't already know?
That life is sad? That this moment
brims with too-sweet wisteria?

And you, too, are sad. And hopeful. Adjustments
were made, the way they can be now.

You pick up your knife and almost
look at it, and put it down again. That she destroys
her life by keeping alive.

Alpine Wedding

All dark morning long the clouds are rising slowly up
beneath us, and we are fast asleep.
The mountains unmove

intensely. And so do we. Meadows
look down.

A city there looks up and
stirs a little. Adrift the rolling tiled roofs of
buildings, the deadly

trains of grinding sand and morning—
a spy unfolds his paper,

the coffee's served.

A bride and groom stand shivering on a tarmac
in the mist, and
they are happy. Each one

and all of us entangled, the room is moist with us,
the house unfinished, windowless,

and we are fast asleep.

The brother of the groom can't get
close enough. He leans against the brightest ridge
and ladder, the sucking

sound of memory
as heaven picks up speed and

hurtles through his burning skin
its frozen blankets
to the sun.

Between Murmur and Glare

Intense and
sudden brooding. Echoing. The ceiling
and the walls and the floor.

Between you and me
the furniture
gives ground. The hills

ease. Horizons
thin to the thin skies of the sea.
As a boat

to the window.
As anxious birds that seem always
to be starving.

On death. And
living. We can talk about living
between

islands.
On paper. Pure
glare. The strung lanterns

cutting into it.
Murmured on terraces. Laughter

in the square.

Like footsteps. Like tourists
streaming toward
evening.

Their shouts are words too.
Page after page of
dark water.

A Waltz for Debbie

As one swept swiftly past, and, lingering still, clings to but can't
        breathe the future. Or like the one who awakens as if
just falling off to sleep again, the dawn turns in its white robe,
        and looks back, and flies to the cold.

In the dream I know by heart, all is forgotten. Everything
        flares there. And is silent. In the shadow that knows me
        better, nothing's
changed, nothing doesn't change here. It's just a room, and the
        freed waters of the sea could talk me into anything.

And so the cliffs, and the wind, and their crowns of twigs are
        islands. A bright horizon, the mere
idea of you, so weirdly high upon the page.

The Vigil

Look again...the fence glistening in overcast light, the grass at
　　　its brightest. Images of no one. Of one's own family,
　　　burying itself. Rust-colored earth, or it seemed that
　　　way—I don't remember.

Old fool, the mask is inside—no one sees through you but me.
　　　And it's winter and pacing, the conversations you'll have,
　　　and the person you speak to agrees.

But listen. Listen...how the living cry out in their cars, in
　　　the stillness of sleep. The lover left out—pure harmony!

My love in the kitchen, paring apples—and why not? why
　　　shouldn't she? The marvel of her hands, her head tilted
　　　that way. Humming to herself, or dreaming, smiling
　　　when she sees me—

what am I that your spirit's a killer!

And So Asks

Scissoring palm trees in the gorgeous light above.
Spires and gold-colored domes.
The blue of the avenue—
the air itself
handed down among crisscrossing
wires and rusted vanes

astonishes with our breathing
the pulse of shadows
and trains.

Blood blossoms the mortar—
newsprint and clutter and the chemical taste
the eye goes to
and savors,

and the stone too looks around.

From that which is not.
From that which is not but used to be and so asks
a stranger to snapshot our leaving—

that you were happy too,
relieved somehow and nicely tired,
and the smoke

and the hillsides drift by.

Silk

This is not
your death book. It's only
glass and light, the heart I taught to think
and thinking I believed that.

If I've
not given you a sign I've taken
to the streets and wandered them alone with you,
and rubbed shoulders
with the crowds.

I need all
the happiness you've
given, your love and scorn for life, the thousand
windows of indifference
and dream.

Cypress make a formal pattern of the statues on the hill.
Waves slap against the sea wall.
I need a radio nearby. Your
dancing. Your
silk.

Dead light of autumn, your
sky is closer to the touch. It's barely April
on my skin.

Tidy

I miss you too.
Something old is broken,

nobody's in hell.
Sometimes I kiss strangers,

sometimes no one speaks.
Today in fact

it's raining. I go out on the lawn.
It's such a tiny garden,

like a photo of a pool.
I am cold,

are you?
Sometimes we go dancing,

cars follow us back home.
Today the quiet

slams down
gently, like drizzled

lightning,
leafless trees.

It's all so tidy,
a fire in the living room,

a rug from Greece,
Persian rugs and pillows,

and in the kitchen,
the light

fogged with windows.

This

Today, my love,
leaves are thrashing the wind
just as pedestrians are erecting again the buildings of this drab
forbidding city,
and our lives, as I lose track of them,
are the lives of others derailing in time and
getting things done.
Impossible to make sense of any one face
or mouth, though
each distance
is clear, and you are miles
from here.
Let your pure
space crowd my heart,
that we might stay awhile longer amid the flying
debris.
This moment,
I swear it,
isn't going anywhere.

From the Balcony

Out there, where whales swim upon a building and muffled
harbor sounds collide. Where trains collide. A perfect
slab of sea upon the specks of those who stroll upon its
shore.

Among the very dawn of us, a single shrug of heart unleashes
waves of birds and voices from the plaza. Then falls back
again. And that much more denied.

One step of yours and cafes steam with coffee. A butcher
parks outside our door. One nod and pots of blue
chrysanthemum explode the blowing day.

Where echoes eat our papers. Real names, the fountains, rows
of sycamore become their feathered haze. In our most
human clothes, along the balustrades of all the gardens,

one breath is pure desire.

THE AUTHOR

Ralph Angel is the author of two previous collections of poetry: *Neither World,* which received the 1995 James Laughlin Award of the Academy of American Poets, and *Anxious Latitudes.* His poems have appeared in *The New Yorker, Poetry, The Antioch Review, The American Poetry Review,* and many other magazines, and have been collected in numerous anthologies, including *The Best American Poetry, The Body Electric, New American Poets of the '90s,* and *Forgotten Language.* His recent honors include a Pushcart Prize and awards from the Fulbright Foundation and *Poetry* magazine. Mr. Angel is Edith R. White Endowed Chair in English at the University of Redlands, and a member of the MFA Program in Writing faculty at Vermont College. Originally from Seattle, he now lives in Los Angeles.